THE
WYNNING
WAY

A Guide to
Creating Success
Your Way

ADVANCE PRAISE FOR

THE *WYNNING* WAY:
A Guide to Creating Success Your Way

"I have watched Maisha Wynn make this journey, and could not have imagined that she could translate it into a practical road map where readers can all walk their own road to greatness. I hate self-help books – this is a story of triumph, rich with self-disclosure and reality…you won't even realize how much you are helping yourself!"

—**Robin Robinson**
  Emmy Award winning news broadcaster

"Purposeful, determined and faithful on the journey - Maisha is an inspiration! As a living example of God's plan for abundant health and vibrant wellness, Maisha's life is a testimony of what can happen when we surrender our meager plans to God's greater will. Maisha's infectious enthusiasm to share her story will bless countless others as they learn to accept themselves as the wonderful and beautiful manifestations of love they have been created to be."

—**Monica Moss**
  First Lady of Trinity United Church of Christ, health minister and life purpose coach

"This insightful book is the veritable blueprint for success! For those who want to win at life, *The Wynning Way: A Guide to Creating Success Your Way* is the perfect springboard for developing the life you imagined!"

—James T. Alfred
    Actor, writer and producer

"Wynn's book will inspire you to make 'getting active' a priority and liberate all of your doubts! The fear of failure is a leading reason why people won't commit to an exercise program. *The Wynning Way: A Guide to Creating Success Your Way* shows us that with hard work, determination and dedication failure is not an option."

—Daniela Spaid
    Director of marketing and public relations, Fitness Formula Clubs

"In reading *The Wynning Way: A Guide to Creating Success Your Way,* I am reminded of a quote by Dr. Benjamin E. Mays, "It must be borne in mind that the tragedy of life doesn't lie in not reaching your goal. The tragedy lies in having no goal to reach." Maisha bravely shares with her readers how she overcame many obstacles, and expertly shows us how we can do the same. Thank you my Spelman sister."

—Raymond Lambert
    Author, producer and social entrepreneur

The Wynning Way™ A Guide to Creating Success Your Way
© Copyright 2015 by Maisha Wynn

Published by Live To Wynn Publishing,
a subsidiary of Live To Wynn, LLC

www.livetowynn.com

ISBN 978-0-692-54573-7
Cover design by Lynnette Galloway
Interior designed and formatted by

www.emtippettsbookdesigns.com

DEDICATION

This book is dedicated to the memory of my beloved mommy and favorite girl,
Sister Sharu.
You have truly been the wind beneath my soaring wings.

CONTENTS

Author's Note

If you are not looking for MORE out of life and living, then this book/journal is not for you. I will kindly return the life investment you've made to purchase this inspirational work. And why? Because this book was conceived and created for women and men who truly desire to make the most of their day-to-day existence—those who are truly ready to turn where they are today, into a greater tomorrow.

This work is dedicated to those who desire to live a rich and vibrant legacy each and every day that they're blessedly given. If you believe this person is you, then please, continue reading with an open mind, a receptive spirit and lastly, a pen. You alone are accountable for what you are about to embark upon. Welcome!

Your sister in faith,
Maisha S. Wynn

CHAPTER *ONE*

Who Am I?

"I am fearfully and marvelously made by God."
~ **Maisha Wynn**

To my family and friends, I am known as Maisha Wynn. However, the outside world knows me best as "WYNN WIN." For me, Wynn (my surname) and win—a homonym of my last name—is no accident at all, because I am truly a born winner.

By the time I was entering the fourth grade, I knew that I wasn't like other children. I was fat. No, not "phat," in the way that means haute couture (i.e. Alexander McQueen to Vivienne Westwood) in the high-end fashion industry, but fat in the way that indisputably means weighing too much.

I can vividly recall a time in my life where I was visible to my family and close friends, but invisible to the outside world. People would walk right past me like I was a ghost. To add insult to injury, even adults would sarcastically tell my mother, "Your daughter has such a cute *face.*"

In school, my peers would taunt me by calling me "Ms. Piggy," or "Fatso." For the average individual (from a child to an adult), hearing such derogatory comments would not only cut deep like a double-edged sword, but scar them for life. However, it left me truly empowered. I know it had a great deal to do with my beloved mother, for she instilled greatness in me at a very young age.

She would always tell me, "Maisha, You are beautiful! You were born to be a leader, and not a follower." Her words held more power and weight than how the outside world saw me.

I knew being uniquely different was not by chance, but design. I had to go through this part of my life to become the woman I am today; one that is confident, competent, courageous and compassionate. Ultimately, allowing me to inspire and impact change in others who might be battling their own personal demons (e.g. weight, family, depression, fear, hate, self-love), I've learned that we must embrace our struggles as powerful tools to make us more resilient. We were built to last, as children of the Most High.

Early in my youth, I knew that I wanted to attend Spelman College, the famed African American women's institution in Atlanta. The women I'd read about there reminded me a lot of the woman I admired all my life, my mother. They had a powerful presence about them and were extremely intelligent. Though she was a single mother, my mother made sure I was able to attend this esteemed institution. She left her entire world in Chicago (including family and friends), to start a new life with me in Atlanta. I mean, my mother was my biggest cheerleader.

In order for me to live the best, she made weighty sacrifices—no matter how major they may have been—so much so that she depleted her entire retirement plan so that I could not only go to Spelman, but graduate. Losing her in recent years was like losing the air you breathe. My once vibrant world felt dark and depleted. For months, all I could do was cry my sadness away. It was too painful to realize she was no longer just a phone call away. My mother was truly my favorite girl and best friend. People who I didn't even know, knew who I was and my story because she was that proud of me.

The unconditional love she showered upon me daily is what keeps me going to this very moment. Her favorite, and most often repeated phrase was: "Do this in remembrance of me," taken from the Bible. Oh, how deeply rooted my mother was.

Regular church attendance was a must growing up in our household. It didn't matter if you had partied and enjoyed a great time the night before; you were getting yourself up on Sunday morning to praise God for what you had been given, and for his blessings. The selflessness she exuded over the years is what constantly propels me to keep moving, keep going, keep living and keep inspiring. But I know very well that not everyone experiences the type of love that I did in my home, where saying "I love you" was ritual, where hugs were a necessity and speaking positively was an imperative.

Now, fast-forward 25 years later. I am the woman I am today because of my beloved mother. Instead of being a part of the scenery, I walk into a room with presence, grace and power. Most importantly, I was able to break the *transgenerational* cycle of obesity which plagued most of my family members— especially my mother who passed away three years ago on New Year's Eve. Losing her to myriad health issues forever changed my world. She was my life-support. Having her make her transition at such a youthful age completely altered how I viewed my life and existence. I became aware of just how truly strong I am during this low point in my life. It was a humbling time for me. Each day I am given life, I am living out her rich and vibrant legacy.

Through trial and error, your confidence is like a golden compass. It's your inner navigational instrument that reflects how you feel about yourself and how you allow others to treat you. The same energy and focus you might use to complete a project for someone else, must be poured back into you—universe (mind), temple (body) and soul (spirit)—especially if you desire to "wynn" at life. Think of yourself as a new structure being built. You must be willing to dig down deep into the soil (your inner mental workings) to build yourself back up.

An architect will tell you that a building site must be completely surveyed to establish the basic footprint of the structure, before any construction can take place. Step one to developing one's "wynning" structure begins with the mind, the greatest gift bestowed upon humankind. Many people have not tapped into this resource because they are not aware of the true power that it holds relative to their existence. As a young woman who was able to transform her eating, living and thinking, I know where the power begins and ends. It starts with the mindset of the man or woman whom you see in the mirror daily; not your loved one, colleague or friend.

> ### WYNNING ACTIVITY:
> Who Are You?

The first step toward creating your own "wynn" begins with you. I know it is easier to focus your energy on the shortcomings of your neighbor, colleague, and/or loved one, but assessing yourself alone is essential for your personal growth. All life journeys include self-reflection and self-awareness. If you desire your tomorrow to be better than today, start your journey now. I discovered that I had to concentrate on my strengths, my energy, my passion, my confidence and my willingness to grow and learn, and you can, too. Taking the time to concentrate on your strengths and weaknesses will only propel your existence.

Start asking yourself life-changing questions, questions that will make you truly dig deep (And please, be honest with yourself). Make note of your answers in the spaces provided below:

1. Am I completely happy with me (Y or N)? Why? Remember, your happiness is connected to your mental peace.

    I'm not all the way there yet because I still need to find out what I want to do for success. And over come these challenges in my life

2. Am I living out my life's purpose? When you wake up daily with a smile on your face, you are living out your life purpose. When money doesn't fuel your drive, it is your life purpose that does so.

_____

_____

_____

_____

_____

3. Do I like what I see when I look in the mirror? This is an exercise you should do weekly. You are what you see. Your self-reflection will make you more cognizant of the situations and/or individuals in your life that are truly holding you back from creating your personal "wynn."

_____

_____

_____

_____

_____

4. How can I love myself more?

By not putting so much pressure on myself. Knowing that I am doing the best I can do and take one day at a time.

"I'm taking my freedom, putting it in my stroll. I'll be high-stepping y'all, letting the joy unfold. I'm living my life like its GOLDEN."
~ Jill Scott

CHAPTER *TWO*

You Were Born to Wynn

"If you want to stand out in life, don't try to be different, but be the 'wynner' you were created to be from birth!"

~ Maisha Wynn

My favorite Hip-Hop lyric of all time is: "All I do is win, win, win no matter what!" The day your Creator formed you, you were born to "wynn," no matter the circumstance or situation. He has already placed within you all of the extraordinary talents and gifts you would ever need to fulfill your calling upon this Earth. In order to understand your calling, you must work on having a personal relationship with Him—one that doesn't revolve around you asking for things, but where you learn the power of listening through a discerning heart. Ask Him to give you the direction He desires for your life. When you recognize His plans versus your plans, you will begin to see your true wins. Jeremiah 29:1 reads: "For I know the plans I have for you," declares the Lord, "Plans to prosper you and not to harm you, plans to give you hope and a future."

When you truly know your purpose, you can live a joyous life. I don't think it's by accident that I was given the last name "Wynn." There is power in one's name. Do you know the meaning of your name? Well, I looked mine up, and

it means joy in Anglo-Saxon. Joy is defined as the happy state tha
knowing and serving your Creator. It is not something that a ma   ....
can create by their own efforts; it takes the power of knowing who you are and
whose you are, "a child of the Most High," to truly tap into your true worth as a
"wynner." In His presence, you will find the ultimate happiness.

WYNNING ACTIVITY:
Focus on You

What brings you joy? What brings you happiness? Over the next seven days,
I want you to focus on joyous and happy thoughts. The things you think, and
the things you write will begin to produce positive energies that will ultimately
impact you, as well as the people around you. Turn off your phone and
television, and dedicate at least 30 minutes toward improving your thoughts.
Remember, those who are dedicated see progress in their existence.

Monday:

_____

_____

_____

_____

_____

Tuesday:

_____

_____

_____

_____

_____

Wednesday:

_____

_____

_____

_____

_____

Thursday:

_____

_____

_____

_____

_____

Friday:

_____

_____

_____

_____

_____

Saturday:

_____

_____

_____

_____

_____

Sunday:

_____

_____

_____

_____

_____

"All that we are, is the result of what we have thought. The mind is everything. What we think we become."

~ Buddha

CHAPTER *THREE*

Mind Your Thoughts

"What do you hang on the walls of your mind?"

~ Zora Neale Hurston

I hang positivity on my wall. I hang peace on my wall. I hang determination on my wall. I hang love on my wall. I hang joy on my wall. I hang abundance on my wall. I hang wellness on my wall. I hang resilience on my wall. I hang faith on my wall. Why? Because I've learned that the greatest gift bestowed upon me is my mind, which I like to call "my universe." The focal point of all things begins and ends with the power you possess in your mind. It is a gigantic open space that holds everything from the smallest idea, to the greatest vision waiting to manifest into something extraordinary.

Everything you think, contemplate and/or reflect upon is responsible for every event that occurs in your life. In the past three years, several scholarly, published studies have proven the health effects of staying mindful of your thoughts, calling it "disposition optimism." One particular piece was written by Michael F. Scheier and Charles S. Carver, titled: *Optimism, Coping and Health: Assessment and Implications of Generalized Outcome Expectancies in Health Psychology*, documenting why optimists do better than pessimists based upon their ability to solve a problem in order to improve their situation in life. Having this ability to create a shift in your mind begins with reconditioning how you think.

Your most powerful thoughts influence your attitude, which ultimately control your altitude in life. Take a look at our most famed and legendary athletes, from Muhammad Ali to Michael Jordan, who have excelled in their professions based on their mental state—before they engaged in their activity. Individuals like these nurtured their universe with thoughts of victory and winning. On a daily basis, you must be cognizant of what you feed your universe, for what you put into your mind is what you'll get out of it. For example, watching television shows that are filled with drama can create chaos in your life. Maybe not on the conscious level, but surely on the subconscious level. Protecting your universe at all times is key to your personal "wynns."

WYNNING ACTIVITY:
Honor Your Gifts

Identify your positive characteristics. Make a list of your assets, including your talents, experiences, skills and anything else that you feel makes you great.

1. Your Talents
   a) A Good friend
   b) Putting things in an order
   c) Cleaning
   d) Cooking
   e) Singing
   f) Making people feel better when down
   g) Dressing
   h) Decorating house

i) ORganization

j) Getting things done

k) sex

2. Your Experiences/Skills

a) Have a lot of Knowlendy

b) Seen a lot of things

c) Strong

d)

e)

f)

g)

h)

i)

j)

k)

3. Your Greatness

a)

b)

c)

d)

e)

f)

g)

h)

i)

j)

k)

After you've created this master list, I want you to review it every morning before you leave for work, and each night before you head to bed. By reviewing these words of power daily, you're reconditioning not only your mental state of mind, but your overall atmosphere. I call this the practice of gratitude.

There is power in what you write and project. In order to make this a "positive hygiene" (anything that makes you live a healthier life) like brushing your teeth, you must commit to doing it for 30 consecutive days. If you miss even one day, you must start over again from the beginning. Staying committed is the difference between a talker, and doer of change.

"What you feed your mind determines your appetite."

~ Tom Ziglar

CHAPTER *FOUR*

Be Intentional With Your Words

"When you speak positive words, you breathe life over your circumstances. The words you speak magnify the situation positively or negatively."

~ TD Jakes Ministries

Have you ever heard the saying: "Be intentional with your time?" Your time is like your words; they can't be taken back once they have been released into the universe. With that in mind, you must choose your words wisely.

The words you utter can either be healthy, or harmful to your overall well-being. As Darren Hardy, the publisher/editor of *Success* magazine, relates: "Words have incredible power. However, they don't have constructive power until they're spoken." When you become intentional with your words, you are truly giving energy to not only what you say, but how you say it. Once you give life to it, you cannot take it back. I learned from my own personal weight-loss journey that there was power in what I told myself I could do when my body felt fatigued. Speaking life into my own existence, kept me going mentally.

As you embark upon this new self-discovery, be mindful of every single word that rolls off your tongue and floats into the atmosphere. "Let no harmful language come from your mouth, only good words that are helpful in meeting the need; words that will benefit those who hear them," Ephesians 4:29. By speaking words that add value and purpose to your life, you begin to truly build up your level of confidence for yourself, as well as those around you. You'll begin to see a shift in how others respond to you based upon what you speak. For every cause, there is a reaction.

> **WYNNING ACTIVITY:**
> Choose Your Words Carefully

Step One: Self-Evaluation Time

1. Do I speak positive words into my life? Do I speak positive words about my future? If not, why don't I? Remember to be honest with yourself.

_____

_____

_____

_____

2. How do I feel when I hear others speak positive words about me?

_____

_____

_____

_____

3. What will people say about me at my Celebration of Life? Once I have made my transition from this world, how would I want people to remember me?

_____

_____

_____

_____

Step Two: Self-Reflection Time

Go to the mirror in your bedroom or bathroom. I want you to stand, look directly in the mirror for a moment and then begin speaking the words you've written about yourself (good, or not so good).

1. How did hearing those words make you feel?

_____

_____

_____

_____

Starting at this moment, speak words that add value, power, purpose, prosperity, greatness, peace, love and victory into your life. Give birth to a "NEW YOU" on this day.

Step Three: Speak Life

Make sure you recite our mantra every morning: "I have the talent, the ability, resources, love, desire, intellect and power to accomplish anything I put my mind to as a child of the Most High! I love me completely!"

"A man's belly shall be satisfied with the fruit of his mouth; and with the increase of his lips shall he be filled."

~ Proverbs 18:20

CHAPTER *FIVE*

Visualize Your Victory

"Visualize this thing that you want. See it, feel it, believe in it. Make your mental blueprint and begin."

~ Robert Collier

O ne of the greatest methods to achieving the life you were designed to live can be found between your ears! Yes, your ears. Your two beautiful, bright pupils hold the power to help you accomplish whatever you desire in life. What you see in your mind is not only manifested in your actions, but also in your thinking and speaking.

If you desire to be a business owner, it begins with your sight. If you desire to be a senior vice president at your corporation, it begins with your sight. If you desire to be a great journalist, it begins with your sight. If you desire to be a world-renowned opera singer, it begins with your sight. If you desire to be wealthy, it begins with your sight. You are literally just a glance away from the life you dream about morning, noon and night. I know it sounds simple, but what you achieve daily has a positive connection on what you spend your time and energy focusing on. Just ask world champion golfer Jack Nicklaus. He proclaimed years ago in a magazine interview the No. 1 secret to his success as a golfer: "I never hit a shot, not even in practice, without having a very sharp, in-focus picture of it in my head!"

While your brain controls nearly everything you do, it does not work alone. Your eyes send a message to your brain through the optic nerve. Once your brain transmits the information, it must break it down and make sense of what you have seen. As you can see (literally and figuratively), what you spend your precious time watching, viewing and reading can either add to, or subtract (i.e. your days, hours, minutes and seconds) from you achieving your greatest potential in life. Those who are truly motivated by success excel for this very reason. They are the captains of their 600 foot vessel. They have a clear understanding of their goals and go after them daily.

WYNNING ACTIVITY:
Create Your Power Board

I want you to spend an entire weekend focusing on you by creating your power board. What is it? It's the ultimate exercise of putting your vibrant thoughts to paper—especially if you desire to live a life of abundance and greatness. Over the past four years, I've personally found tremendous triumph in my life by creating one. Seeing my goals daily brought me steps closer toward achieving them. I said I would create lifestyle experiences to empower people, and guess what? I have done six empowering series' over the past two years.

What you'll need: A poster board, markers, magazines, glue sticks, and scissors. Now, what you don't see, are images of "YOU." I want you to personalize your power board with images of yourself to bring life to your plan of action. Yes, we are taking the journal and making it truly interactive, like a real "wynner!"

Action Step 1: Leaf through your magazines and cut out positive and progressive words and images which resonate with your spirit and soul. This board is a reflection of you, and where you truly desire to be in life.

Action Step 2: Peruse the images and begin to lay them onto the board. Remove any images that no longer feel right. This action step is where your second sight comes in. As you lay out the pictures on the board, you'll get a sense of how the board should be balanced out.

Action Step 3: Paste everything onto the board including your favorite images of you. Add sayings and writings if you desire.

Action Step 4: Place your power board somewhere where you can see it frequently. Why? Because each morning and evening, you are going to spend at least ten minutes focusing on your montage. I want you to connect with the images and words. Allow them to jump off the board and into your brain.

Putting your desired achievements before your eyes is just one "wynning" key to achieving your goals. There is true greatness in what you observe and watch on a daily basis. Just like it's essential to fuel your temple properly for it to work at optimum condition, the same applies to what you see.

"Your imagination is your preview of life's coming attractions."

~ Albert Einstein

…So, get the popcorn and stay ready!

CHAPTER *SIX*

Treasure Your Temple

"He who loves the world as his body, may be entrusted with the empire."

~ Lao-Tzu

Five months after my late mother made her transition, I met my cousin in Dubai. Traveling internationally was the best decision ever. This exotic, scenic destination turned out to be a space of healing and spiritual awakening for my temple, universe and soul. During my visit, I had the pleasure of visiting the largest mosque in the world, the Sheikh Zayed Grand Mosque. Its opulence was truly breathtaking. Since it was a sacred place of worship for thousands of Muslims, they had certain guidelines in place for visitors like myself who weren't dressed according to custom.

For women, proper attire to enter the mosque meant being completely covered from head to toe. When I reflect back upon this monumental moment in my life, I know that one's body—more appropriately your "temple"—is a place of worship as well. One's temple is where their mind, spirit and incredible wisdom is housed. When you cherish your temple, you are mentally guided to take care of it like a newborn baby. You will love it unconditionally, feeding it foods that give it life. You will push it to new limits by trying new activities that get your heart rate pumping. You will give it rest when it needs it. You'll nurture it by doing things that bring it joy and happiness.

When you cherish your temple (body), you cherish your universe (mind)! Your temple responds to the way you think, feel and act. This is often called the "mind/body connection." Your personal freedom comes from living a healthy lifestyle. Nourishing your temple with the proper foods gives you the energy and fuel needed to propel in every aspect of your being (from how you move to how you interact with others). Psychologist and mindfulness author Jon Kabat Zinn writes, "For the most part, we eat with great automaticity and little insight into its critical importance for us in sustaining life and also in sustaining health." You must learn to slow down from autopilot and be aware of what you are eating. Start cherishing your temple by eating to live, versus living to eat.

There are three "wynning" ways you can truly start treasuring your temple: 1). Be conscious of how certain foods make you feel. Does what you eat impact your temple in a positive or negative way? 2). Pay close attention to your food as you eat it. Are you able to digest it smoothly or is it sitting on top of your stomach, giving you heartburn or making you gassy? 3). Track the times of day when you eat, and your portion sizes. We live in a world where more is greater. However, when you eat often, you don't need to eat more.

WYNNING ACTIVITY:
Write Down What You Consume

I know this is going to be a process for many. However, once you've made up your mind that you are a "wynner," you'll be ready to elevate your life, climb into the driver's seat and take full control of your well-being. As a responsible driver, you must be cautious of the food you put into your temple. You must start by visualizing how certain foods make you feel after you've digested them. Do they make you feel electrified like the bunny rabbit in the Energizer battery television commercials? Or, do they leave you feeling lethargic like a sleeping cting for ten to fifteen minutes, I want you to write down the names of these foods, creating two columns: "Energized Me" vs. "Exhausted Me." This is where the power of seeing becomes crucial as a safe driver.

In order to get from destination A to destination B, you need to fully see your current situation. Next, I want you to go to your refrigerator and pantry and discard everything that you know will only hold you back from reaching your new goal. Performing this important exercise will let your brain know you've moved on via your actions.

Food Journal:

Monday:

Breakfast_____
Time:_____

Snack 1:_____ Time:_____

Lunch_____
Time:_____

Snack 2:_____Time:_____

Dinner_____
Time:_____

8 ounces of Water Intake:_____

How Did I Do Today?
A, B C, D, F (Circle One)

Tuesday:

Breakfast_____

Time:_____

Snack 1:_____ Time:_____

Lunch_____

Time:_____

Snack 2:_____Time:_____

Dinner_____

Time:_____

8 ounces of Water Intake:_____

How Did I Do Today?

A, B C, D, F (Circle One)

Wednesday:

Breakfast_____

Time:_____

Snack 1:_____ Time:_____

Lunch_____

Time:_____

Snack 2:_____Time:_____

Dinner_____

Time:_____

8 ounces of Water Intake:_____

How Did I Do Today?

A, B C, D, F (Circle One)

Thursday:

Breakfast_____

Time:_____

Snack 1:_____ Time:_____

Lunch_____

Time:_____

Snack 2:_____Time:_____

Dinner_____

Time:_____

8 ounces of Water Intake:_____

How Did I Do Today?

A, B C, D, F (Circle One)

Friday:

Breakfast_____

Time:_____

Snack 1:_____ Time:_____

Lunch_____

Time:_____

Snack 2:_____Time:_____

Dinner_____

Time:_____

8 ounces of Water Intake:_____

How Did I Do Today?

A, B C, D, F (Circle One)

Saturday:

Breakfast_____

Time:_____

Snack 1:_____ Time:_____

Lunch_____

Time:_____

Snack 2:_____Time:_____

Dinner_____

Time:_____

8 ounces of Water Intake:_____

    How Did I Do Today?

    A, B C, D, F (Circle One)

Sunday:

Breakfast_____

Time:_____

Snack 1:_____ Time:_____

Lunch_____

Time:_____

Snack 2:_____Time:_____

Dinner_____

Time:_____

8 ounces of Water Intake:_____

    How Did I Do Today?

    A, B C, D, F (Circle One)

Look at your list of intake. Did you honor your temple? Did you honor your spirit? Did you honor your universe? Did you overindulge because if felt good? Did you consume just to be part of the crowd? Did you participate in a habit that you know did not honor your universe, temple and spirit? Did you overcompensate in any way? Did you overconsume salt? Did you overconsume sugar? Did you overconsume processed foods? Your temple responds to everything you put in it. It will maximize its energy, cell development, cell rejuvenation, and waste elimination when your intake is balanced and complete in nutrients.

Respect your temple, universe and spirit by making one positive change next week in your food and drink consumption. Consider having seven fewer cigarettes. Consider drinking eight glasses of water each day. Consider having one meatless meal each day. Consider eating more leafy green vegetables. Consider having breakfast each and every day. Consider having one less glass of wine at dinner time. I call this eating not as if there is no tomorrow, but eating as if there is a tomorrow.

"I finally realized that being grateful to my body was key to giving more love to myself."

~ Oprah Winfrey

CHAPTER *SEVEN*

The Power of Prayer

"Prayer is not asking. It is a longing of the soul. It is daily admission of one's weakness. It is better in prayer to have a heart without words, than words without a heart."

~ Mahatma Gandhi

Who is the source of your power? As a spiritual woman, my continuous source of power comes from God. According to the Holy Bible, the power of prayer is the power of God, who has the ability to hear and answer our prayers. Through prayer one has the ability and capacity to change their heart and transform their existence. For me, it's a loving connection between my higher power and myself. I know I can go to my Creator completely flawed and not be judged. He loves you and me just the way we are. In this life, I've learned that praying first thing in the morning truly gets you centered and focused before tackling the outside world and its elements.

When you come across certain spirits, you want to make sure you are shielded with the grace and mercy of the Most High. Through prayer is where you will find the joy, strength and guidance you need to keep your spirit fueled throughout the day. Don't ever take this time for granted. It should be a part of your daily routine, like breathing or taking a shower. Spending one-on-one time with your Creator strengthens your spiritual muscles while allowing you to give thanks for your many blessings. When you truly have a relationship with your Creator, sometimes just saying "Thank you Father," or "Lord, I need you now" is more than sufficient because our Father just wants to know he has your heart. When you understand that nothing else matters but the glory of God, you will begin to see a major shift in your life and well-being. Next level living is something we should all strive for…like we do earthly possessions.

If you desire healing and peace for the wounds you've carried internally, seek prayer. Your Creator is able to provide for all of your needs and more. However, you must live your life according to his will. Saying His name isn't enough. You must learn to treat others the way you desire to be treated. Love thy mother and thy father. Be a blessing to others. Honor the Lord's name. Put a smile on someone's face by being kind. Speak life into the hearts of others. Start praying for those who have wronged you. Be consistent in your conversations with the Creator. He desires to have a close connection with you.

> ### WYNNING ACTIVITY:
> Your Creator's Time

Starting tonight, I want you to begin an intimate conversation with your Creator (morning and night). If you wake up during the night to use the restroom, stop first and thank your Creator for giving you life. I've learned that how you start your day is how you should end it. You want to have your spirit fed completely before dealing with the outside world.

Here are some of my favorite scriptures for you to recite while spending time with your higher power:

1. Philippians 4:6-7: *"Do not be anxious about anything, but in everything by prayer and supplication with thanksgiving let your requests be made known*

to God. And the peace of God, which surpasses all understanding, will guard your hearts and your minds in Christ Jesus."

2. Luke 11:9: *"Ask, and it will be given to you; seek, and you will find; knock, and it will be opened to you."*

3. 1 Thessalonians 5:16-18: *"Rejoice always, pray continually, give thanks in all circumstances; for this is God's will for you in Christ Jesus."*

4. John 15:16: *"You did not choose me, but I chose you and appointed you so that you might go and bear fruit—fruit that will last—and so that whatever you ask in my name the Father will give you."*

5. Psalm 46:10: *"Be still, and know that I am God!"*

Action Step: Apply each one of these scriptures to your life by writing them down on a postcard or index card and placing it in your wallet or purse. When you feel overwhelmed, I want you to pull them out, and recite the words out loud. If you feel the power of the verse, share it with one person each day. Please share below how you felt:

My feelings after reciting _____ scripture:

I felt _____

_____

_____

My feelings after reciting _____ scripture:

I felt _____

_____

_____

My feelings after reciting _____ scripture:

I felt _____

_____

_____

My feelings after reciting _____ scripture:

I felt _____

_____

_____

My feelings after reciting _____ scripture:

I felt _____

_____

_____

"Don't pray when you feel like it. Have an appointment with the Lord and keep it. A man is powerful on his knees."

~ Corrie Ten Boom

CHAPTER *EIGHT*

Create Your Circle of Power

"You are the average of the five people you spend the most time with!"

~ Jim Rohn

Your daily encounters determine your level of success as a business owner, friend, family member and/or executive. Those closest to you will have the greatest impact on you and your fortunes, whether you are aware of it or not. Think about the individuals you spend the most time with, either face-to-face, or on the telephone. Their effect on your character and behavior can either propel your journey in life, or stifle your growth towards greatness. As an only child, I am a living witness.

During my childhood years, I would often daydream about having an identical twin sister; a sibling who not only looked like me, but someone with whom I could share my deepest secrets, who was trustworthy, able to talk about boys, and a faithful partner to work with on school projects. However, reflecting back 20 years later, I know that my biggest blessing was my mother. She had a major effect on my self-esteem, the decisions I made throughout my professional career and my global perspective on life. As my biggest supporter, she was a faithful sounding board. I could always depend on her honesty, nonjudgmental responses and constant support. Individuals like my mother are the types of "wynners" you need in your circle, as you propel yourself toward uncharted territories.

By assembling your circle of power, you are ultimately taking control of your outcomes. You hold the platinum key to unlock a world of endless opportunities. Think of creating your circle of influence like solving a fractional equation where getting rid of certain denominators totally changes the course of your existence. By subtracting and adding certain individuals to your power circle, you begin to assemble a strong alliance with individuals (from family to friends) who share common goals.

Who should you subtract? Those who are toxic to your mind. These are individuals who never have anything nice to say, are overly critical of what you do and always angry about something or someone. Ultimately, people who drain the life out of your living spirit. And whom should you add? Those who genuinely want to see you excel, are always uplifting and can find the greatness in life. These are individuals who pour love, life and joy into your spirit. Researchers have found that being around happy people may be contagious. Psychologist James H. Fowler studied 5,000 people over 20 years and learned that happiness benefits other people through three degrees of connection that can be passed down through your circle of influence.

> ### *WYNNING ACTIVITY:*
> Select Your Friends Carefully

Selecting your friends with care will either allow you to thrive or wilt. With that in mind, reflect upon the individuals you spend the most time with (both professionally and personally). Write down their names, characteristics and how they make you feel. After you have completed this part of the activity, take a hard look at each individual. Analyze each name. If the person is toxic, it is time for you to make changes in your life. You don't need to be around anyone who is trying to infect you with their problems or personal pain. Begin to separate yourself from them. If they confront you, be honest about your feelings and hold your ground.

1. _____ (Name)

_____
_____(Characteristics)

_____
_____(How do they make you feel?)

2. _____ (Name)

_____
_____ (Characteristics)

_____
_____(How do they make you feel?)

3. _____ (Name)

_____
_____ (Characteristics)

_____

_____ (How do they make you feel?)

4. _____ (Name)

_____

_____ (Characteristics)

_____

_____ (How do they make you feel?)

5. _____ (Name)

_____

_____ (Characteristics)

_____

_____ (How do they make you feel?)

"People are like dirt. They can either nourish you and help you grow as a person or they can stunt your growth and make you wilt and die!"

~ Plato

CHAPTER *NINE*

Your Greater Begins With You

"You must be great to yourself first, in order to be good to the universe!"

~ Maisha Wynn

M aterial items are replaceable, but you are not! When you are great to yourself on a daily basis, you can be good to those around you. Nurturing your temple is an active way of enhancing your quality of life and lifestyle—the way you think, move, sleep, eat and interact with others. It's more than taking a quick coffee break between a meeting, or going to get your hair done at the salon. It is taking authentic time away from the outside world to restore, replenish and rejuvenate your inner spirit and being.

When I formerly worked in the advertising arena, I found it to be extremely stressful based on hitting a quota monthly. I would take a mini-vacation four times per year to love on me. I always went someplace warm where I could sunbathe during the day, and visit a spa in the evening. For true relaxation, I would turn off my mobile telephone and read an inspirational book to get my brainwaves flowing. I know it might be challenging for some to disconnect from society, but rest assured the world will go on with, or without you.

Research conducted by Experience in Motion LLC revealed that those that engaged in self-care as an organizational strategy not only improved the healing experience for themselves, but it improved their business measures. Nancy O'Brien, co-founder and CEO of EIM, relates, "The research revealed that self-caring is a fundamental tenant of any organization's culture." When we take great care of ourselves, we are able to improve not only our personal lives, but our professional lives.

Parker J. Palmer, famed author and writer, wrote: "Self-care is never a selfish act—it is simply good stewardship of the only gift I have, the gift I was put on earth to offer to others. Anytime we can listen to our true self and give it the care it requires, we do it not only for ourselves, but for the many others whose lives we touch." I've learned that it is our God-given responsibility to nurture our temple. It is where everything is housed from our special talents which make us unique, to our major vital organs that keep us alive. Taking care of our temple as well as our universe are vital to our overall well-being. Your car doesn't operate on empty, does it? A lack of not taking care of you puts not only you in danger, but those you love.

WYNNING ACTIVITY:
Respect Your Greater Self

Note: Since nurturing oneself is very unique based upon one's personality, this is all about what brings you happiness and peace of mind.

Next, you are going to write out what you will do over the next week. Remember this is all about you—not your loved one, best friend and/or colleague. Spend some quality time with just you. This can be walking along the lake, getting a 30-minute aromatherapy massage and/or just sitting somewhere quietly with your eyes closed and breathing. I am positive this is an activity you will continue to do long after finishing this book.

Monday:
_____
_____
_____
_____
_____

Tuesday:
_____
_____
_____
_____
_____

Wednesday:
_____
_____
_____
_____
_____

Thursday:
_____
_____
_____
_____

Friday:

_____
_____
_____
_____
_____

Saturday:

_____
_____
_____
_____
_____

Sunday:

_____
_____
_____
_____
_____

"When you recover or discover something that nourishes your soul and brings joy, care enough about yourself to make room for it in your life."

~ Jean Shinoda Bolen

CHAPTER *TEN*

You Are Your Personal Brand

*"Your brand is what people say about you
when you're not in the room."*

~ Jeff Bezos

Once upon a time, the term "brand" was commonly used when describing a FORTUNE 500 company, but in the world we live in today 'you and I' are brands —— personal brands to be exact. Years ago, *Fast Company* magazine published an article on personal branding that stated: "Regardless of age, regardless of position, regardless of the business we happen to be in, all of us need to understand the importance of branding. We are CEOs of our own companies: Me Inc. To be in business today, our most important job is to be head marketer for the brand called You."

Living in today's digital world, individuals can find you in seconds online just by "Googling" your name. According to an AVG study, 92 percent of children under the age of two already have a digital footprint online. With that in mind, you want to guard your personal brand for dear life because you value and cherish it. Major global enterprises like Starbucks and Estée Lauder understand that the golden rule for a successful brand begins and ends with protecting it. They are able to maintain credibility through consistency in their message and delivery whether you are in Chicago, or Paris. The stronger the brand, the greater the connection is to consumer experiences. This intangible part in a business plays a major role in sales and trust.

As a walking billboard of life, you are no different than Starbucks or Estée Lauder. The playing field is now level, and like a major enterprise you want to establish credibility with your audience. How others perceive you go hand-in-hand with how you present yourself to the world. Your personal brand and reputation are interchangeable. The mental impression you leave on the minds of those who meet you can offer two things personally and/or professionally: 1). Open new doors of opportunity for growth and expansion. 2). Close new doors of opportunity for growth and expansion. Why? The moment others see you, their mind has already started calculating if you are trustworthy, honest and confident. And these calculations are made at the blink of an eye, or more acutely in less than seven seconds.

First impressions, whether good, bad or indifferent, are influenced more by nonverbal cues (from one's personal style, body language and facial expressions) made by an individual, than by social exchange through words. Studies have shown these cues have over four times the impact on the impression versus what one projects from their mouth. With that in mind, positive impressions can be made through the way you present yourself as a brand. Coming from the world of sales and marketing, I understand the power of nonverbal cues. I've closed more business deals face-to-face versus over the phone. There is true power in a client having the ability to be able to see and connect with your personal brand. Oftentimes, I would show up with no appointment like I was supposed to be there. I'd walk into a building tall and poised, dressed to the nines from head to toe, and knowledgeable about the client's product or service. I understood the power I possessed with a client experiencing me personally.

Proper care, attention to detail and being consistent with your message are a must when creating your brand. I want you to spend time analyzing various media outlets (from TV commercials, to magazine and Web ads and radio commercials). Replicate a page or two from brands that resonate with your universe and spirit by observing how they are able to tap into the audience you desire to reach.

Three things you will look for while critiquing them:

1. *Their creative.* What market are they trying to reach? How were they able to captivate your attention immediately?

_____

_____

_____

_____

_____

2. *Their message.* Do they have a compelling story? Look for engaging and intriguing content which connects with your emotions.

_____

_____

_____

_____

_____

3. *Their selling point.* What benefit(s) are they offering which can positively enrich your life? What is your need for the product?

_____

_____

_____

_____

_____

"Branding demands commitment; commitment to continual re-invention; striking chords with people to stir their emotions; and commitment to imagination. It is easy to be cynical about such things, much harder to be successful."

~ Richard Branson

CHAPTER *ELEVEN*

Give Thanks Daily

"Thank you is the best prayer that anyone could say, I say that one a lot. Thank you expresses extreme gratitude, humility, understanding!"

~ Alice Walker

Gratitude is truly the cornerstone to your greater self. How? To have the ability to see a new horizon is golden to your life span on this earth. We must honor our Creator, by showing our appreciation through our actions. Waking up with a big smile is the first way to give thanks. Each morning, I am able to embark upon a new day, I must spend some time giving thanks through my prayers. I've learned your joy in life comes from your overflow, which is powered by your outlook on life. How you view and respond to certain situations daily sets the tone for how the universe will treat you.

1 Thessalonians 5:18 reads: "Give thanks in all circumstances, for this is God's will for you in Christ Jesus." Learning how to embrace and express gratitude (to be thankful) completely on good days and not so good days is an essential part of one's personal growth (mentally and spiritually). It activates positive emotions in your brain. The positive emotions you awaken can create a peaceful environment allowing you to embrace the spirit of gratitude. The

ability to train your universe with statements that embrace thanks like "giving honor to God" or "truly blessed" will start to activate favorable emotions to your brain. Your level of appreciation shows your desire to be the very best you! You no longer feel like the victim in life, but take on the role of a victor. You no longer feel alone, but connected. You no longer feel depressed about your life, but hopeful. When you fully acknowledge an attitude of gratefulness, you will experience multiple spirit-filled shifts in your subconscious mind.

WYNNING ACTIVITY:
Gratitude to Greatness

To begin bringing gratitude into your world, I want you to close your eyes and reflect on all of the people, situations and circumstances that have brought you pleasure (big and small). Tap into all your senses from the smell from the day, what you wore, the sounds around you, what did you say and did you give them a hug to say thanks. Now, write it down:

Gratitude 1:_____

_____

_____

_____

_____

Gratitude 2:_____

_____

_____

_____

_____

Gratitude 3:_____

_____

_____

_____

_____

Gratitude 4:_____

_____

_____

_____

_____

Gratitude 5:_____

_____

_____

_____

_____

Gratitude 6:_____

_____

_____

_____

_____

Gratitude 7:_____

_____

_____

_____

_____

Gratitude 8:_____

_____

_____

_____

_____

Gratitude 9:_____

_____

_____

_____

_____

Gratitude 10:_____

_____

_____

_____

_____

You have so much to be thankful for in life. I want you to come back and revisit this chapter whenever you feel down, discouraged and/or overwhelmed. Seeing is truly believing.

BONUS ACTIVITY:

Take a few minutes and write a thank you letter to someone in your life, or someone you have lost in this life, that has been a blessing, and whom you have not properly thanked. This can be a co-worker, or a close friend. It doesn't have to be lengthy, but make sure you're specific about what this individual did, and how it affected you and your overall spirit.

Wynning Homework:

1. Mail your thank you card if the individual is out of state. However, meet them face-to-face if they are in the same city with you, and read the note card out loud to him/her.

2. Start keeping a gratitude journal. I want you to put your thoughts on paper so you can see daily just how blessed you truly are when challenging life lessons begin to surface in your life. Remember, your hurdles are not meant to break you down, but to strengthen your spiritual muscles.

"Reflect upon your present blessings, of which every man has plenty; not on your past misfortunes, of which all men have some."

~ Charles Dickens

CHAPTER *TWELVE*

Forgiveness Is Freedom

"Forgiveness is not an occasional act;
it is a permanent attitude."

~ Dr. Martin Luther King, Jr.

I have learned the hard way, that being hurt as a result of a bad situation, or poor decision making is painful and shameful. The reason it is painful and shameful is my inability to see pain as being caused by my own poor choices, actions and judgment. In other words, it is easy to blame my pain on others. It is easy to blame my shame on the conduct of someone else. If she hadn't... If he hadn't... If only he had... If she just would... These are the things we say to ourselves when we feel pain, or shame.

I have learned the hard way that if I can look at my own actions, my own conduct, my own mistake in judgment, my own decision making and my own thoughts, I would find things that I would do differently. Once I forgive myself for my actions, decisions, judgments and words, then I can forgive the other person involved in the equation. Self-forgiveness begins with honesty and self-truth.

Anger is real! Pain is real! Hurt is real! When you've been broken by negative words, false promises and abusive situations by someone you trusted and loved, it can impact your happiness and inner peace. Why? Those inner scars can lead to strong negative feelings known as resentment. Pain is the mother of anger, and the father of bitterness. Mentally holding on to these emotions will not only suppress your growth, but your state of mind. Your ability to forgive and let go is not about the other person, but more about YOU! How you choose to handle your past will have an impact on your tomorrow. Your emotions play a preeminent part in the process.

The "how" and "why" lead to how your future will play out. Psychologists proclaim mustering up genuine compassion for those who have wronged you, instead of allowing anger toward them to eat away at you, is the course of action to take. Making the choice to let go is an extremely powerful step towards restoring your heart. It is a slow, steady process like learning how to ride a bike for the first time. You get on with a determined spirit. You might stop and start due to the learning curve. However, with time, you begin to ride looking straight ahead with confidence. Take your time and know that small steps lead to big results. I am speaking from personal experience.

For many years, I was a walking volcano ready to erupt. To the outside world I may have appeared picture-perfect, but on the inside I was miserable and battling inner peace. Not having my father in my life truly hurt me. My personal feelings of abandonment turned into resentment. When my peers would ask about my father, I'd say he was deceased because in my heart he was dead. He left my mother with the burden of paying for my college tuition when he could have assisted.

These poisonous feelings had a major impact on my relationships with men. Whenever a gentleman would try to take our relationship to the next level emotionally, I would personally sabotage it by being confrontational. Why? I was fearful of him walking out of my life, which prevented me from building a healthy relationship based on love and support. This destructive cycle went on for years, until I was able to release myself from my own personal bondage.

Forgiving my father was about me liberating myself. It was the greatest gift I could have given myself; the ability to live free from anger and resentment.

If you truly desire to live a life of my THREE "WYNNING" P'S: peace, power and purpose, you must learn to FORGIVE those who have wronged you through their actions or words. It is not about giving in, but about healing your own spirit. Creating a spectacular life for you is the best form of positive payback. You must continuously remind yourself, you are most like your Creator when you forgive. Releasing the emotions that you have been holding onto for a week, or even years, will open up new opportunities for growth. The universe will notice a transformation in your energy. You will begin to think more clearly, smile brighter and shine with joy.

> *WYNNING ACTIVITY:*
> Reflect and Release

The reflection you see daily is what you present to the world. Reflecting back upon your past allows you to "feed your soil," also likened to strengthening your inner peace. Once you begin working on a better you, you'll start to see a change in your inner health. Start by forgiving yourself.

Action Step 1: Go somewhere quiet and sit on the floor with your legs crossed. Bring with you your journal, and a pen.

Action Step 2: Get focused by taking a few deep breaths. Begin by breathing through your nose and exhaling through your mouth. (You are going to spend some time reflecting on your past).

Action Step 3: Now, close your eyes and focus on one individual who has hurt you mentally, physically and or emotionally.

<u>Action Step 4:</u> Think about that moment when it occurred. Where were you? How did it begin? What words were exchanged? Did you scream? Did you cry? Really dig deep.

<u>Action Step 5:</u> Now open your eyes. Be conscious of how you are feeling at this moment. Release tears if you must. It is a cleansing experience.

<u>Action Step 6:</u> **Turn to page 78 (RELEASE SHEET)** - Write out answers to the following questions:
1. Who hurt you? Name the person who hurt you.
2. What pain did they cause you? Be as detailed as possible.
3. What about the situation hurt you so deeply?
4. How is this person and situation blocking your true happiness in life?

<u>Action Step 7:</u> Analyze the answers you've written out. Look at them. Next, close your eyes and ask your Creator to release the pain and resentment you are feeling.

<u>Action Step 8:</u> Say with conviction: "I am letting go. I desire true peace in my life." Do this each night before you go to bed for the next 21 days.*

*Research shows that it takes 21 days to develop a habit.

"Forgiveness is the key to action and freedom!"

~ Hannah Arendt

CHAPTER *THIRTEEN*

Invest in Others

"When you focus on being a blessing, God makes sure that you are always blessed in abundance."

~ Joel Osteen

You have one life! What you do with it on a daily basis will have a major impact on your future. If you ask anyone who is a philanthropist, they will tell you that investing in others is one of the greatest feelings, whether you donate your time, talent and/or tithe. It should come from a personal space of not expecting any recognition. Your biggest reward is knowing that you've made a difference in the life of someone other than yourself. The Holy Bible proclaims: "Be generous, invest in acts of charity. In return it will yield high returns." When you give unconditionally from your heart, it adds value to your existence.

Over the past two years, my company has given back to the community in a big way (from arts education programs, to helping women get back into the workforce). The feeling after we have been able to help were truly gratifying to my spirit, and soul. To see the bright smiles of those we have touched is truly priceless.

Being a blessing to others can also help take your mind off what you might have going on in your own world. A Gallup survey on volunteering in the United States found that Americans who actively work to better their communities have a higher overall well-being than those who do not. Why? It allows you to see the impact you can make by helping someone else who's less fortunate, especially when you see them standing strong in the midst of their own storm. This relationship between one's well-being and giving back shows how interwoven the connection of assisting others is. It's just as important to your health as exercise, and eating right.

The more you invest in others, the more you grow as an individual. You begin to gain a new perspective on life by being of service to the world. You start to understand that life does not revolve around you. When you give to others unconditionally, the world smiles back at you.

WYNNING ACTIVITY:
Be of Service

Action Step One: Find out what you are passionate about and invest your efforts. Here are a few ideas to get you thinking:

1. Donate clothes, shoes and other possessions to organizations like The Salvation Army, or Goodwill.
2. Volunteer your time at a women's shelter.
3. Volunteer to help at your children's school.
4. If you enjoy being active, train and participate in a local 5K, 10K or other race that gives back to a charitable organization.

Action Step Two: Make a commitment to be of service within the next 30 days. The sooner the better.

Action Step Three: Please fill out the following after you serve:

1. What nonprofit organization did you bless with your time, talent and/or finances?

_____

_____

_____

2. How did it make you feel after giving back?

_____

_____

_____

_____

_____

3. Will you continue what you've started? Yes or No? Why?

_____

_____

_____

_____

"What counts in life is not the mere fact that we have lived. It is what difference we have made to the lives of others that will determine the significance of the life we lead!"

~ Nelson Mandela

CHAPTER *FOURTEEN*

Throw Away Your Fears

"Fear is only as deep as the mind allows!"

~ Japanese Proverb

Fear and success are counterintuitive. The two nouns should never be written or uttered in the same sentence. Fear is described as an unpleasant emotion caused by the belief that someone or something is dangerous, likely to cause pain or a threat. The only threat success has is when you permit your universe to doubt your God-given talents and abilities.

Many of us have hopes and desires for more in life, whether it's personally or professionally, but worry about the uncertainty of the "HOW" factor. When you allow a powerful emotion like fear to stop you from reaching your greatest potential in life, you are not living out the desires and dreams bestowed upon you at conception. Instead of living your purpose, you are spending your time and energy on negative thoughts.

Imagine how powerful you would be if you overcame your fears? If you replaced your doubt with dedication! If you replaced your fear with God's favor! Through self-awareness, you begin to take action. Don't resist or deny it, but focus on what might be triggering it. Is it a fear of complacency? Is it fear of feeling you are unworthy of more in life? It's essential that you identify what is holding you back from achieving your greatest. Billionaire investor Warren Buffet had a fear of public speaking, but he knew that in order for him to be a truly successful businessman he had to overcome his fear. Buffett took action by taking a Dale Carnegie course. Moral of the story: Today is just temporary. Tomorrow is one step closer to victory. When you combat your fears by being mindful of your purpose, you emerge bigger and better than where you are today. It's easier to ascertain what you desire and deserve.

> ## WYNNING ACTIVITY:
> Tear It and Toss It

Take five minutes and reflect upon your fears in life—large and small. **Write them down on page 79** of your journal. I want you to visually SEE what's holding you back from reaching your greatest in life as a "WYNNER." Also, I want you to recite them audibly so you can hear what is holding you back as a BORN "WYNNER." Take one last look at the sheet of paper. Tear the sheet out of your journal and toss it in the garbage. This ACTION is very powerful because you are ridding yourself of emotions, people, things and/or habits that have been detrimental to your overall well-being.

1. How did this exercise make you feel? (Reflect before you respond.)

_____

_____

_____

_____

"Face your fears and doubts, and new
worlds will open up for you!"

~ Robert Kiyosaki

CHAPTER *FIFTEEN*

Explore the World

*"The world is a book, and those who don't
travel read only one page!"*

~ St. Augustine

W hen you travel outside of the country, you truly give purpose and power to your life. It will forever change the way you look at yourself and the world. I speak from personal experience as someone who obtained her first passport at the age of 11. It was one of the greatest gifts my beloved mother could have given me. As a single mother who was an educator, she wanted more for me. As a result, she invested in my greater by elevating my universe.

Children who start traveling at an early age will garner the wisdom and knowledge of a lifetime. The ability to learn another language, or to embrace a culture outside of our own is invaluable to our personal growth. I can still recall the experience of my first international trip to Cuba (from the humidity of the air, to not having running water with which to bathe each day). Spending the summer in another country taught me there are much greater issues in the world than my own current situation. Never again will I take running water for granted.

Traveling will transform you like little else can. It is great for you. The benefits of exploring the globe are both mental and physical, the result of "physical activity, cognitive stimulation and social engagement," according to a study commissioned by the U.S. Travel Association. You will love the personal journey and freedom that comes with traveling outside your personal space. Stepping into new surroundings and scenery will only liberate your soul and broaden your universe, as you create a lifetime of memories for yourself. You will be drawn to wondrous experiences, cultures, history and people which will forever transform your thinking.

You will not come back the same man or woman you were when you left. Observing firsthand how other people live outside of your home city or country will challenge you to be the change you desire to see in our world today. When you look back over your existence, you will have one-of-a kind memories to keep you smiling. I still think about a trip I once made to Indonesia. I took my mother there for her birthday. We went to art museums in Nusa Dua, and cherished our temples by getting massages right on the shores of the Indian Ocean.

The attraction about traveling the world is that there is no preferable way to travel. Don't put any limits on it. Just make sure you travel boldly. Travel freely. Travel far and wide.

> ## *WYNNING ACTIVITY:*
> Plan Ahead vs. Putting It Off

Taking time away from your career can be truly gratifying. However, many people easily come up with reasons why they can't travel like "they don't have time" or "don't have the resources" for experiences that will bring them peace, love, clarity, happiness and knowledge. Before you know it, another year has gone by with no vacation. To make sure this doesn't happen, I want you to do the following. Review the checklist that follows.

Check List:

1. Purchase your passport, if you don't already have one.
2. Put in your vacation request with your supervisor. If you work for yourself, note it in your Outlook calendar. Planning is key to making this happen.
3. Now do some research on where you'd like to travel. You can consult loved ones and friends, as well as "Google" some results based upon things you enjoy doing.
4. List your top five destinations:

A._____

B. _____

C. _____

D._____

E._____

5. Narrow it down to one. Price or level of interest might be factors.
6. Start putting aside money in a special fund, or hire a travel agent who can set up a special payment plan.
7. Live abundantly on this day - TRAVEL.

"Travel, in the younger sort, is a part of education; in the elder, a part of experience."

~ Francis Bacon

CHAPTER *SIXTEEN*

Start Loving You

"You yourself, as much as anybody in the entire universe, deserve your love and affection."

~ Buddha

Have you ever heard the poignant statement: "You can't love another person till you love yourself first?" Well, I'm here to tell you that this is 100% true. Our Creator is LOVE through and through! As a man or woman created in his image, you are a very special individual. There is no other man or woman in this world quite like you. God invested his best when he conceived you. As his child, you deserve to be loved not only by those in your circle of power, but by the most important person ever—YOU!

When you are genuinely compassionate and kinder to YOU, you will feel buoyant internally. You become extremely conscious and mindful of everything you do whether it's who you are dating, or how you treat your temple. As a young lady who battled her size most of her life, I never knew that I was obese until I looked at old pictures. However, I knew I wasn't completely happy because I wasn't completely comfortable with me (from how I looked or felt). Over time, I realized that I was doing myself a huge disservice so I took action as opposed to putting it off. It was a process, but one that has been so enriching to my life.

The University of Michigan researched the well-being of Americans, and reported that the best predictor of general life satisfaction was not satisfaction with family life, friendships, or income, but satisfaction with self. The best way to exercise "love for self" is to learn who you are as a human being—what you like, what you don't like, what makes you happy, what makes you sad, what motivates you to excel in life and more. When you honestly are able to take a look inside of yourself and have a conversation with your Creator, you start to embrace self-love and compassion by acknowledging who you were destined to be.

Happy people are compassionate towards their own feelings. They don't have an issue with taking ownership for their success or shortcomings. For example, if they work on a project and it doesn't turn out favorably, they don't beat themselves up. Instead, such individuals learn how they could do it better the next time. People who love themselves have enough courage to take action for who they are and learn from every situation, without placing blame or allowing it to keep them down. It shows a level of appreciation for oneself. They know there is a joy in every sunrise, hope in every situation and progress in every crooked path.

> *WYNNING ACTIVITY:*
> 7-Day Love Challenge

Spend some quiet time by yourself. Tune in to how you're feeling inside and try to be at peace with who you are. Over the next seven days, I want you to write down what you love about yourself. It can be about how you perform at work, to how you are a blessing to others by volunteering. I want you to visually see the greatness which is inside of you.

Monday:

I love_____

_____

_____

Tuesday:

I love_____

_____

_____

Wednesday:

I love_____

_____

_____

Thursday:

I love_____

_____

_____

Friday:

I love_____

_____

_____

Saturday:

I love_____

_____

_____

Sunday:

I love_____

_____

_____

"The most powerful relationship you will ever have is the relationship with yourself."

~ Dr. Steve Maraboli

CHAPTER *SEVENTEEN*

Your Ears Hold Power

"You are what you listen to!"

~ Unknown

Your choices in life define whom, and what you become. Many people often take what they hear for granted. However, what you hear can influence the way you think, act and feel which has a major impact on the quality of your life. And why? Well, quite frankly, hearing has a significant connection to your surroundings. Your ears serve as an essential function, allowing you to connect with the sounds produced by your environment. Music, words, and sounds are all forms of communication, which evoke various emotions followed by your reaction. They all speak to the core feelings and sub-consciousness of your spirit.

Music is a language of instinctive feelings. Words are a language that expresses one's ideas and thoughts. Sounds are an unspoken language traveling through the air as sound waves. As you reach higher plateaus in life, being forever mindful of what you listen to involves taking the necessary steps of cutting out forms of communication which are not fruitful to your life. Researchers at the University of Groningen discovered that music is not only able to affect your mood, but listening to particularly happy or sad music can even change the way individuals perceive the world.

There is a connection between one's character, lifestyle, who they speak with daily and their choice of music. As I've gotten closer to my Creator, I've had to make some serious changes in what I listened to on the radio, as well as television shows I consumed. I grew up in the early era of rap music, however the current state of the industry has shifted. Consequently, I have changed my musical preferences to Jazz and Gospel. They fuel my universe with positivity and power. Jazz music engenders an intimate connection between myself and the storytelling being played by woodwind instruments, while gospel music fuels my soul with love from its uplifting words.

That same type of positive elevation I feel from music is what I work towards being around daily, from the people I engage in conversation, to the type of programs I watch on television. When you are intelligent about what you listen to, you gain a better sense of self and your overall mood improves. How you identify yourself is shaped by what you hear. Selecting the "right" forms of communication in the right scenario will enable you to live a life of intent, and purpose.

WYNNING ACTIVITY:
Nurture Your Ears

You truly are what you feed your universe. The average American listens to four hours of radio per day. For one week, I am challenging YOU to a fresh beginning. Your assignment is to spend time listening to CD's, Internet radio and/or videos on YouTube from some of the world's most sought-after inspirational leaders, from Deepak Chopra and Bishop T.D. Jakes, to Oprah Winfrey and the Dalai Lama. These are just some examples, but watch individuals who are where you desire to be in life. Use their words as a positive springboard to propel you to where you want to be in life. Commit to at least 15 minutes of listening per day.

1. How did you feel after making this change?

_____
_____
_____
_____
_____

2. Did you notice a shift in your mood? If so, in what way?

_____
_____
_____
_____
_____

3. Were you more productive? If so, in what way?

_____
_____
_____
_____
_____

"Pay attention to what you're hearing! You will be evaluated by the same standard with which you do your evaluating, and still more will be given to you."

~ Mark 4:24

CHAPTER *EIGHTEEN*

An Active Heart Is a Healthy Heart

"Physical fitness is not only one of the most important keys to a healthy body, it is the basis of dynamic and creative intellectual activity."

~ President John F. Kennedy

Your longevity starts with your heart! It's one of the most vital components to living a healthy lifestyle. Most of us want to feel healthier and stronger, but never seem to have enough hours in a day to commit to being active. When you make yourself a priority and put in the work, there is no greater feeling.

Over the years, I've learned that 20 percent of what we feel and look like begins with getting active. Physical activity is one of the best life investments you can make towards this goal. My personal transformation was not an overnight success. It took over ten years to reach my personal goal, as I put one foot in front of the other. My "yo-yo" mentality made it a long, winding and arduous process to hit my marathon life goal. There would be days when I felt like working out, while other days I would put it off completely. It was not a top priority for me. However, my breaking point came when I reached a level in life where I was sick and tired—tired and sick of how I felt. With your personal freedom not only comes liberation, but a new lifestyle. A style of life that includes doing, feeling and living better.

Being active doesn't mean you have to join a gym to begin a routine. Simply making the mental commitment to start, followed by small changes can have a major, positive impact on your health. Research has demonstrated that virtually all individuals can benefit from regular physical activity, whether they participate in a vigorous exercise program, or some type of moderate health-enhancing physical activity. You can literally walk, mop, run and/or swim your way toward living a more joyous existence. These activities will control your weight, strengthen your bones and muscles, reduce your risk of some types of cancer and Type II diabetes and ultimately prolong your life. I don't know about you, but I want to live as long as Sarah did in the Holy Bible. Not to mention, you'll have more energy to enjoy life with family and friends. Your overall way of life will transform right before your eyes.

WYNNING ACTIVITY:
Make Being Active a Lifestyle

Reflect upon various activities that you took delight in as a child. Did you enjoy dancing, roller skating or swimming? These are all excellent workouts that can get your heart rate up, as well as burn calories. Once you've figured out which activity you'd like to do, plan it below. Now, find an accountability partner to assist you in achieving your goal. The individual should be motivating, willing to confront you if need be and willing to follow up on the personal commitment you've made with them. Let them know what new fitness goals you are taking on, and which days you are going to work out.

I will work out on the following days of the week:_____

_____

To make it official, fill in the blanks herein and e-mail your new accountability partner, stating: "I, _____, am committed to working out _____ days (at least 30 minutes per day) a week for the next 30 days. I will commit to giving it my very best—even when I don't feel 100%! This is truly my time to nurture me completely and fully love the King or Queen I was destined to become."

Lastly, pick a day and time you will follow up with your accountability partner.

"Movement is a medicine for creating change in a person's physical, emotional, and mental states."

~ Carol Welch

CHAPTER *NINETEEN*

Plan to Wynn

*"Setting goals is the first step to turning
the invisible into the visible!"*

~ Tony Robbins

W hether you desire to be the President of the United States, or a *New York Times* best-selling author, setting goals is a building block to long-term success. Clearly stated goals and objectives are your personal road map to progress and prosperity! Seeing them written out on your laptop, or in a journal will allow you to visually see what you need to accomplish. I learned from my business mentor, Bill Walsh, that one should routinely write out new goals to be achieved every 30 days.

It's all about transforming your daily habits. Each month, you should have a list of new goals you will tackle as well as a plan for how you'll complete them. Also, setting up a system to measure your goals is just as important as knowing them. For example, if you want to improve your health, you should have a way of keeping track of your gains. Doing this will make you consciously articulate your desires, which will ultimately give new meaning to your destiny.

Reaching your goals is like breathing for survival. When you list them, you're motivating yourself to turn a possibility of being great, into a reality of living greatly. A 1979 study done with students attending The Harvard Business School supports this "wynning" theory. Graduate students were asked to set clear, written goals for their futures and how they planned on accomplishing them. To that point, only three percent had written goals and plans, 13 percent had goals but they weren't written down and the remaining 84 percent had no stated goals.

Ten years later, they were interviewed again. Thirteen percent of the class who had specific goals, but had not written them down earned twice the amount of the 84 percent who had no goals, while the three percent who had written goals were earning ten times more than the other 97 percent of the class combined. As you can see demonstrated here, setting a specific goal and seeing it through daily will help you manifest the things you desire in life. There is value in the visible.

WYNNING ACTIVITY:
Set Your Life Goals

Write out seven new goals you desire to reach over the next 30 days. Next to each goal, write your action steps to achieve your goals. They can be professional, or personal goals which you have been putting off for one reason or another.

Goal 1:_____

_____

_____

Your Action Step:_____

_____

_____

Goal 2:_____

_____

_____

Your Action Step:_____

_____

_____

Goal 3:_____

_____

_____

Your Action Step:_____

_____

_____

Goal 4:_____

_____

_____

Your Action Step:_____

_____

_____

Goal 5:_____

_____

_____

Your Action Step:_____

_____

_____

Goal 6:_____

_____

_____

Your Action Step:_____

_____

_____

Goal 7:_____

_____

_____

Your Action Step:_____

_____

_____

_"If you set goals and go after them with all the determination
you can muster, your gifts will take you
places that will amaze you."_

~ Les Brown

CHAPTER *TWENTY*

Accountability Always Wynns

"As iron sharpens iron, so one person sharpens another."

~ Proverbs 27:17

W e're all accountable for our actions, thoughts and words! Those like myself who believe in next level living, know the power of someone else holding you accountable, whether it's increasing your business or your dedication to eating healthier. With the right people and frequency in your life, you are more mindful to stay on track. The act of accountability serves to assist you along your "wynning" path to move forward.

Your accountability partner is someone who ensures that you stick to the goals you've determined for yourself. Ultimately, they take on the role of a trusted advisor who can provide positive and critical insight, while encouraging you every step of the way. He or she will motivate you when you need the strength, pray for you when you need to hear a word from your Creator and celebrate your victories no matter how large or small. An interesting study was done that surveyed a group of individuals. The outcomes were illuminating. Those who had an accountability partner to review their goals throughout the year with them had a 75 percent or better chance of reaching them, versus those who had no partner.

I've been on my healthy lifestyle journey for years. As much as I'm very self-motivated, there are times I need someone in my corner to give me an extra push. Having a personal trainer as part of my arsenal of living well has paid off tremendously. We meet every week at the same time and days, and we work together toward my personal goals of being stronger and achieving a more sculpted physique. For me, knowing there is someone there to hold me accountable adds pleasant pressure, and assures me that I am making myself a top priority…even when my world becomes too hectic.

Do you have someone like this in your life who motivates you to excel and offers guidance? It could be a family member, a loved one, professional colleague and/or someone in your power circle. This individual should be dependable, positive, driven and trustworthy. To make sure they are in alignment with your passion and personality, you need to interview them the same as you would someone watching after your children or elderly parent. Your new level of success begins now!

> ### *WYNNING ACTIVITY:*
> Accountability Time

In the previous chapter, you wrote out your goals. Now it's time to put them to action by selecting the proper accountability partner. Create two-to-three questions—based on your needs; e.g. personal, professional and/or financial —for them to ask you, and three-to-five questions to ask him or her. You are both interviewing each other to see if this is a good fit, like a new pair of shoes. A sample interview question could be: What motivates you in life? Remember, the more in-depth the questions, the more you'll find out.

Question 1:_____

_____

_____

Question 2:_____

_____

_____

Question 3:_____

_____

_____

Question 4:_____

_____

_____

Question 5:_____

_____

_____

Question 6:_____

_____

_____

Question 7:_____

_____

_____

Question 8:_____

_____

_____

"Accountability breeds responsibility."
~ Stephen Covey

WYNNING ACTIVITY:
Release It
---

1. Who hurt you? Name the person who hurt you.

_____

_____

_____

2. What pain did they cause you? Be as detailed as possible.

_____

_____

_____

3. What about the situation hurt you so deeply?

_____

_____

_____

4. How is this person and situation blocking your true happiness in life?

_____

_____

_____

WYNNING ACTIVITY:

Unleash Your Fears

Author's Thank You Note

Thank you so very much for journaling with me. It was a pleasure to share my journey with you. I pray each activity gave you insight on how you can improve your life. Your time is NOW.

Until we connect again, continue to stay on your "wynning" path of self-discovery.

I love you,
Maisha S. Wynn
www.livetowynn.com

A Round of Applause

An African proverb reads: "It takes a village to raise a child." I am truly thankful for my village. They were very instrumental during the birthing process of my vision.

This book/journal would not have been possible without the support of Ronald E. Childs, Rashida Mathis, Darlene Paris, Karen Williams, Clint Evans, Melvin Brooks, Danyele Davis, Shelley Cooper, Jacqueline Jackson, LaKerie Williams, Scoop Jackson, Quita Lockley, Craig Baylis, Kimberley Rudd, Tracey Burns, Gavin Jackson, Cathy Gault, Marguerite Malloy, Javin Foreman, Cortni Harris and my entire "wynning" network.

- Maisha S. Wynn